The EZ Guide
To Successfully
Achieving Your Goals

By:

Cynthia A Copenhaver

Certified Neuro-Linguistics Practioner, Life Coach, Hypnotist

Table of Contents

Introduction

Many people on this planet devote a lot of time to deliberating their long term and short term goals. Almost everybody wishes they could snap their fingers and instantly those changes would magically occur in their life.

Whether it's regarding their life with their spouse, children, friendships; romantic relationships, career or money, everyone wishes to change something. The primary step that will do that is certainly to set goals.

Even so, many people are experts at 'wishing' to set goals; unfortunately many are practically 'unfit' motivationally and knowledgeably to follow through on those wishes.

How often have you chosen a goal and basically didn't follow through? You were all excited at the prospects, then just did not know where to begin or you began making excuses to yourself and others why you could not get to it at this time. Seem familiar?

That is essentially considered the 'norm' for many. The

easiest method of confirming this fact would be to think of each new calendar year.

The largest component of New Year's celebrations is not the get-togethers; it is in reality in all the resolutions.

We all choose to attend and converse about quite a few New Year's Eve events, the most usual direction of all conversations are regarding the resolutions we are going to fulfill in the coming new calendar year.

The main problem is that most people have is that they set identical resolutions each year, and on a yearly basis, they are unsuccessful. After all, if most of us were triumphant; why would we keep making identical resolutions yearly?

This book was created to teach you the best way to end the actual constant replay of the same resolutions on a yearly basis. Basically it will likely be your all-inclusive guide in helping you in setting, fulfilling and maintaining all of your goals in each and every aspect you could imagine.

When I actually say every part you could imagine, I really mean every part you could ever wish or want. Aren't you actually getting bored with trying to struggle on your own and constantly finding you have to do that again every other month?

This EZ Guide will help you creatively establish goals for:

- Personal / Professional Relationships

- Work

- Finances

- Personal physical fitness and health

- Spiritual Growth and more

By realizing your goals you can:

- Achieve more within your lifetime

- Improve your present performances

- Increase your motivation and determination skills

- Increase your self-esteem and satisfaction with achievements

- Improve your self-confidence

- Lose limiting attitudes/beliefs that hold you back and cause disappointment

People who use goal-setting proficiently and strategically:

- Suffer less from panic and anxiety disorders

- Concentrate more and are more self-aware

- Have improved self-esteem

- Perform better in all of the areas of their life

- Are happier and even more satisfied

Setting Goals Facilitates Self-Confidence

The skills for achieving your set objectives and experiencing their achievement will offer you the confidence and the belief in yourself. This will place you in a position to pursue higher levels of your dreams in your future goal setting.

By adhering to the section on goal setting and the action plan chart which offers you effective guidelines to help you to take advantage of this technique efficiently. Goal setting is relatively simple, providing that you have the self-discipline and motivation.

How To Select Your Goals

Setting up goals alone seriously isn't the exclusive challenge you are going to face. From time to time, choosing suitable goals for starters is the tougher aspect. You can choose to start with any goal you feel is needed for your wellbeing, stability or happiness.

Goal setting is only an official process to get personal planning. By listing your goals using a general outline list, you select what you desire to achieve, and then transfer a step-by-step manner to chunk this down into manageable tasks that you can achieve successfully.

Having the tools for setting goals and tasks means that you can choose where you intend to go with your life. You are in complete control. By discovering exactly what you really want to accomplish, you figure out what you should concentrate on specifically. You also realize and understand what your resources are and what your limiting distractions may be.

Goal setting is usually a standard technique utilized by professional athletes, successful business owners and great achievers in a variety of fields. It gives you long term vision and provides you with short term motivation and determination.

It makes sense to give your attention and understanding direction, which really helps you to organize your resources. By means of setting exact and well defined objectives, you will be able to measure and take pride from the achievement of your goals. You will observe forward growth in what might until now have seemed like unnecessary work.

Structuring a successful goal:

Goals usually are set on several unique levels. From the start, you choose what you want to do with your wellbeing and what large range goals you intend to achieve.

Then, split these into the smaller chunked down steps you need to hit in order that you reach entire lifetime ambitions.

Finally, upon having your step ladder for success, you take action towards achieving it!

Establishing Goals: Plan of Action

The 1st step in all personal goals is usually to consider what you desire to achieve in your lifetime, as your lifetime goals offers you the perspective which shapes all aspects within your decision making process. Just imagine what you really would like to achieve in various areas of your life.

To help provide you a variety of areas that you could imagine, try to align your goals within the following areas:

- Artistic:

  Would you like to achieve any artistic goals? If so, what would they be? Do you intend to write a poem; paint on canvas, or generate musicals, start your own band, or create a novel, etc?

- Attitude:

  Does your individual mindset limit you from earning more? At this time, is there any way you behave which upsets you, do you talk an excessive amount? Are you pessimistic? Are you too sociable or an isolationist? If so, make improvements to your habit or find a solution to your challenges.

- Career:

What level would you like to reach with your career? Will it be your goal for being the employer of your own company, or change career fields and begin another more fulfilling pathway for yourself?

- Education:

Is there any knowledge you intend to acquire or some type of study that you wish to pursue? What knowledge and skills would you need to achieve these pursuits?

- Family:

Would you like to improve your parenting skills? How to be more sociable in family or friendly gatherings? Spending more quality time? Start your own family?

- Financial:

How much would you like to earn? At what age? What would you do for making that take place? How about savings? Retirement Goals?

- Physical:

What are your athletic goals you intend to achieve, or are you interested in good health and fitness well into your senior years? What steps should you take in achieving this?

- Pleasure:

How would you like to enjoy you? You should be sure that some goal you could have is aimed toward making yourself happy, content, or abundantly joyful. Really visualize yourself accomplishing that goal, imagine the pleasure it will bring to you and others when you are successful.

- Service

Would you like to make the earth a much better place by your existence? How? Everyone has some effect on the world and others around them to some degree.

Just a simple smile and frown from you to a passerby can begin a chain reaction effect. So imagine, what you could accomplish by taking control of your life and achieving your set goals successfully.

In having decided ones plans around such various areas, you need to assign importance to them to succeed. Then critique the goals and re-prioritize unless you are satisfied that they reflect the design of the life you'd like to achieve.

Also, be sure that the goals are definitely the goals YOU want to achieve, and not what your parents, significant other, family, friends, or employers want.

Success exclusively happens while you're working for your own personal well-being because undergoing it for other people will ensure that you sabotage your own success before you even begin your journey.

Achieving your Goals

Once you've set your goals, the ideal thing you can do is establish a schedule of chunked down tasks you need to complete for you to reach and fulfill your lifetime plan.

From there it is possible to just shorten your entire goal spans as an illustration, you place a 5 year plan, 1 year plan, 6 calendar month plan, and 30 days plan of progressively smaller goals/tasks that you need to reach to perform your long term goals.

Finally set a day-to-day to do chart and list things that you have to do today to work towards your daily life goals.

Once you have chosen what your first range of plans would be, keep the job going by simply reviewing and updating the to-do list on a regular basis. This allows you a chance to boost your self-confidence, rewarding yourself and is a perfect way to confirm you are making progress.

You really have to periodically review the long term plans, and change any issues to reflect your current changing focal points and experiences in your lifetime.

Everyone should be using the previous plan. It is the ultimate way to begin to perform a lifetime that may be fulfilling and leads to a life without constant strife with failure.

You watch, by beginning slowly, you are giving yourself the chance to realize, understand and handle achieving goals that you only could dream about in the past.

Nobody truly succeeds in attaining a goal that was forced though. In hastening through and planning to achieve the goals quickly, you will likely miss a small number of key aspects which might really alter your conclusion. Take your time and really consider your goals, resources, and limitations. You may have to successfully remove a limitation in order to achieve that lifetime goal. Follow through completely.

You may achieve momentary success quickly, but if you don't take the time to correct your limitations…you will find yourself facing more difficult challenges and will struggle to maintain that success. It will be a hollow victory.

By following the correct process, you will find that challenges are no longer bothersome and may even seem more exciting. I know at this point, you may find that difficult to believe. Honestly, I guarantee with success, your confidence soars!

Establishing Goals:
Effectively

There is a difference in setting goals and setting them effectively. Anyone can set a goal, but doing it effectively means that it will actually have a successful outcome. There are many things that you can do, but if you don't know how to begin, you are stuck.

The following guidelines will help you to set effective goals and help you manage your time in an efficient manner that will cause your goals to become fact.

Express your goals in a positive way. That is a key component to setting goals you can attain.

How often have you been excited to accomplish something that didn't even sound positive when you spoke of it afterwards? If you are not comfortable or happy with the goals you have set, the likelihood of you succeeding is pretty low.

In order to express your goals in a positive way, you simply must first think of a goal that puts a smile on your own face when you imagine it completed. Why would you desire to set a goal that made you frown, cringe or be sad?

When you are beginning to set your goals it helps when you are talking about them to others in a manner that states your actions as positives because it will have others seeing it being a positive as well.

That will guarantee you more support. In the end, don't we all need a little support when we are attempting to do something positive in our lives?

Be specific

Create a specific goal that includes starting dates, times and amounts so you can properly measure your achievement.

If you do this, you will know exactly when you've achieved your goal, and can take complete satisfaction from successfully achieving it.

Being specific in setting your goals is only creating them with exact and precise details. It is easier this way because then you can certainly follow a step-by-step format. That's all there is to that.

Prioritize!

When you have multiple goals, give each a certain priority. You will avoid feeling overwhelmed by way too many goals. This helps direct your attention to the most critical goals and allow you to follow each in succession. Setting priorities will force you in to the step-by-step format above.

By doing the most important first and moving towards the least important in succession, you're enabling each task to be easier than the last. It causes the accomplishment of each task to be easier and easier, which will encourage you to complete the multiple goals.

Write goals down

Writing them down crystallizes your goals and offers them more force. You are better able to successfully maintain your scheduled tasks for each accomplishment. It also helps you to remember each task which should be done and allows you to check them off as they are accomplished.

Basically, you can better keep track of what you are carrying out so as not to repeat yourself unnecessarily.

Chunk the tasks down

Keep the low-level goals you are working towards small and an easy task to achieve. If a goal is too large, then it can seem that you are not making any progress towards it. By chunking down those larger goals into smaller manageable tasks you will have more opportunities for reward. Derive today's tasks from larger goals. It is a great way to accomplish your goals.

Focus on performance, not outcome

You should take care to set goals over which you have as much control as possible. There is nothing more dispiriting than failing to accomplish a personal goal for reasons that are beyond your control.

These could be bad business environments, poor judging, bad weather conditions, injury, or just plain bad luck. If you base the goals on your own personal performance and resources, then you can keep control on the achievement of your goals and get satisfaction from achieving these.

Be Realistic

It is important to set goals you can achieve. All sorts of people (parents, media, and society) can set unrealistic goals for you and this is almost always a guarantee of failure. They will often do this in ignorance of your personal desires and ambitions or flat out disinterest.

Alternatively you can be naïve in setting very high goals. You might not appreciate either the obstacles involved, or understand quite how many skills you must master to accomplish a particular level of performance.

By being realistic you are boosting your chances of success.

Do not set goals too low

Just as it is important not to set goals unrealistically high; do not set your goals too low. Some people tend to do this when they are afraid of failure or when they simply don't want to do anything at all.

You should set your goals so that they are slightly in your immediate grasp, but not so far that there is simply no hope of achieving them. No one will put serious effort into achieving a target that they believe is unattainable.

However, remember that your belief a goal is unrealistic may be incorrect. If this could be the case, you can change this belief by using images or visualizations of you successfully achieving this goal quite effectively.

Achieving your Goals

When you have achieved success, you have to take the time to enjoy the satisfaction of experiencing the reward of accomplishment. Absorb the implications of the goal achievement, and observe the progress you get towards other goals.

Even if the goal was insignificant, you should reward yourself appropriately. Think of it like this, why would you choose to ignore any accomplishments that you get?

In doing that, you are downplaying your accomplishment

which will convince the critical part of your brain that it wasn't that important to start with.

With the experience of having achieved each goal successfully, you should next review the others and see them in the pursuing manner:

- If you achieved your goal too easily, be honest with yourself and make your following goals more challenging.

- If your goal took a disheartening length of energy to achieve, make the next goals a little easier. Perhaps, you need to chunk it down more.

- If you learned something that would cause you to change your other goals, make those changes and establish new goals. This is growth.

- If while achieving your goal you noticed a specific lacking in your skills or resources, decide which goals to set so that you can fix this.

You should keep in mind that failure or experiencing challenges to meet goals does not matter so long as you learn from it. Feed lessons you learn, back into your goal-setting system.

You must also remember that your goals will change as you mature. Adjust them regularly to reflect this growth in your personality. If an original set goal no longer holds any attraction for you in your new view on life, let them go.

Goal setting is your servant, not the master. It should bring you real pleasure, satisfaction and an expression of successful achievement. Remember you have complete control over your life choices and decisions. Most limitations you think are stopping you, from going forward, are only minor steps that you will resolve and step over to achieve your goals successfully.

Set up a To Do List of tasks to do tomorrow to move towards your goals. When you do, you will soon realize you will be on your way to using your goal setting on a routine basis.

Key Points: Setting your Goal

Goal setting techniques are an important method associated with accomplishing any lifetime achievement. Nevertheless, there are some key points that you ought to consider before setting your objectives.

- Deciding the most important thing for you to achieve and making your choices based on your knowledge or experience.

- Separating what is important from what is irrelevant. This means that your focus will be in the correct place.

- Motivating yourself to achievement to make sure of achieving your goal.

- Building your self-confidence with the achievement of your set goals

- Ensuring that your goals are your own

This should allow you to ultimately enjoy the achievement of your objectives and reward yourself appropriately. You have to learn lessons when they don't work and feed these back into your plan strategizing. In learning through mistakes and errors, you will be guaranteeing future success.

Many believe that there would be more than five tips to goal setting, but truly you will find only five. Everything else is simply a branch of the primary five points.

The following diagram will show you the key points in achieving your goals. It shows what results from the key points in the setting of your goals.

If you continue to include more branches to those 4, you will see that they all are manifestations of what you happen to be seeing. As you continue to add more branches you will discover that all these things will tie to the first branches.

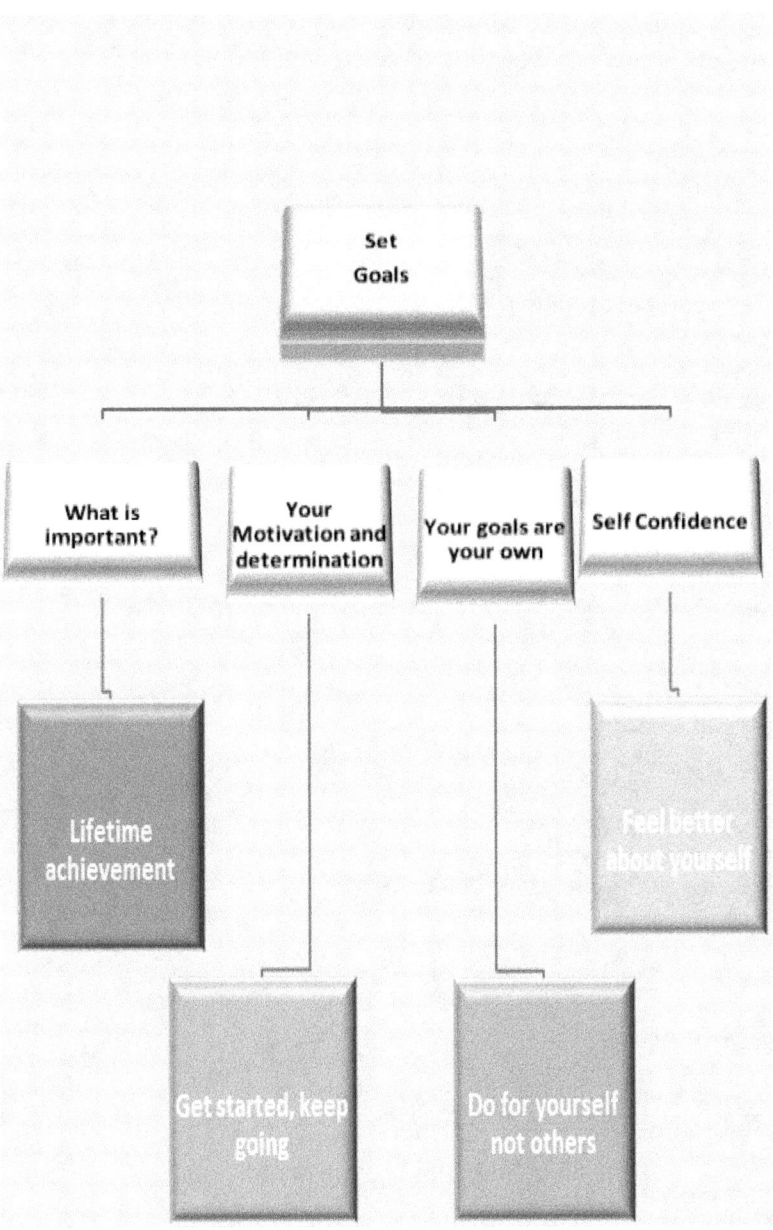

What Could Go Wrong?

Goal setting techniques can go wrong for several reasons. When these things occur, it can be devastating towards your self-esteem and can silence the thought of setting any new goals.

Before you can look into what you should do about solving these types of goals setting challenges, let's see what these can be. This section is really a more detailed explanation from the previous section, but I felt that this is a needed section of its own.

If it seems repetitious, it is! But it is extremely necessary for this guide; specifically for quick referencing later.

Outcome goals can be set, rather than performance goals. It forces you to pay attention to the end result immediately, rather than taking your time to undergo the steps of goals placed. When you set goals properly you'll be doing it in a step-by-step manner. Where you are utilizing outcome goals, you fail to offer the goal reasons outside your own control, this can be very dispiriting and can result in loss of enthusiasm and emotions of failure. Always set performance goals instead, as this provides you with a higher chance of being successful.

Goals can be set unrealistically higher. When a goal is perceived to become unreachable, no effort will be produced to achieve it. Set realistic goals to be able to best decide how to start achieving them.

Goals can be set so low that you simply feel no challenge of advantage in achieving the goal. Setting goals is a waste of time. Always set goals which are challenging enough to be worth your time and effort, but not out of your achievement reach.

Goals can be so vague that they're useless. It is difficult to understand whether vague goals have already been achieved. If an achievement can't end up being measured against your expectations, your self-confidence will not benefit from goal setting techniques, nor can you observe progress towards a larger goal. Set precise, specific and quantitative objectives. Try to make it real enough it would fit in a wheelbarrow!

For example: You want to get and education...what kind? You need to narrow down your target goal so that you can actually see the specific aspects of your goal! An education won't fit in a wheelbarrow...but a specific study course or book will fit, or a yoga class may be added.

Goal setting can be unsystematic, infrequent and disorganized. In this case certain goals are going to be forgotten, and the achievement of goals won't be measured and feedback will not really occur into new goals. The major advantages of goal setting have been dropped. Be organized and regular in the manner that you use your plan of action for set goals.

Too many goals that aren't given priority might be set, leading to a sensation of overload or burn out. Remember that you deserve time for you to relax and enjoy being alive and never solely focused on your objectives and achievements.

By avoiding these difficulties, and setting goals effectively as described in the earlier section, you can achieve a stronger forward leap towards your successful future dreams.

Getting Specific

Although the concept of setting goals in general is a good one to learn; which was explained previously, it helps everyone set goals in specific areas in your life, separately.

For example; if you need to better your health or lose weight, you'll be setting goals that specifically focus on your health. Of course, health and fitness goals aren't the only goals that many people are looking to set. Other regions of goals include:

- Career / Financial

- Relationships

- Family

- Spiritual

- Social/cultural

Let's check out all of the most common goals that you ought to consider.

What will be the point in learning how to create goals in general and not really give specific examples and instructions on the most typical goals that are set? Let's begin now.

First of all what do you consider stops most people from achieving what they need out of life? Perhaps it's a lack of talent, knowledge, lack of ability, personal circumstances, and upbringing. I'll let you know this much; it's none of these.

The single biggest reason people have is an inability for reaching goals is motivation, or not setting them to begin with or not wanting to take the time.

If you don't start, then how can you be prepared to move forward? Many a prolonged adventure started with the littlest of steps. Action is the initial step to achieving your goals.
Many people are fine at choosing a goal to create, but are inept at achieving them. You can achieve all you want by taking one action.

One step is all you have to make. One step today, one step in a few days or tomorrow, whichever is easier for you. The important thing is to keep making steps after you have started.

The trouble is, often the initial step is the hardest, and the next step is just as difficult. It is only once you have made a series of steps does it actually get easier.

You need to understand the truth about what is actually holding you back. Motivation and goal setting go together. The goal is your journey and also the motivation is your fuel to make it happen.

You may have many objectives, but no fuel to make it happen. You may have gallons of fuel, but then have no set journey to take.

What can prevent you from having that journey? There are a lot more things holding you back than you understand.

YOU are probably the greatest cause. The way you approach an objective will ultimately affect whether you'll achieve it or not. The good thing is that you can break free of whatever limitations are holding you back.

Friends and family are following in line. They may have your very best interests at heart, but often their own inaction is actually what lies behind their advice for you.

It is really common for all those around you, to hold you back, since they are not doing anything on their own. For example, if you are reducing your weight, some in your support group or friends will inadvertently sabotage you by offering you food or unhealthy snacks.

I'm not saying that all advice is bad, it's that sometimes the most well intentioned comments can empty your own fuel can faster than a vacuumed siphoning hose.

You need to spot this stuff when someone or something is actually draining your fuel and stop it, either mentally or actually break free of whatever is holding you back. Now that you know this particular, let's get started.

Strategies to Developing your Action Plan

• Create your goal (being specific and positive)

• Strategize backwards from your original goal

• Face your fears and expectations

• Write your Plan down and put it into action

Your own goal planning a career move is similar to mapping your route for a road trip. If you don't know where you are going, you can't decide on ways to get there. If you do know where you are going, you'll get there quicker. Goals like "Go back to school" are too general and never specific enough. You have to translate these types of goals into specific statements for example "Enter a college accounting plan by next fall" or "For the following two months, search for work within the computer securities field." You need to know exactly what you want to complete and when to go about this.

Planning backwards is one of the very best ways to move forward. Start by asking yourself if you're able to accomplish your goal today. If you can't, why do you consider that is? What do you need to do first? Is there something you need to do before that? Keep thinking backwards until you arrive at tasks you can do today. This will enable you to attain the goal's starting stage.

For example, if your goal would be to take a two-year business management program, could you start today? No, you have to be accepted towards the program first. Could you end up being accepted today? No, you need to apply first. Could you utilize today? No, you have to determine which post-secondary institutions to apply to. Could you decide today? Absolutely not, you have to do some research first and so forth. I could do this all day long but you get the idea. Don't worry if your list of things you can do becomes several lists.

Deal with your fears and expectations of yourself immediately when realized.

Look over your list of things you'll have to do to achieve your objective. Do you believe that you can do it? If you have uncertainties, take some time to believe them through first. Are your own expectations realistic? Have you succeeded or been unsuccessful at tasks that were similar to this before? What can you do to enhance your chances of success this time? What resources do you have available already? What do you need to accomplish this task?

For example, if there is a great chance you will not follow-through with your plans, you need to ask yourself why. Are you a professional procrastinator? If so, what can you do to make certain that you will keep going before you reach your goal? Are you a person afraid of failing? If that's the case, work at improving the skills you'll need. Or test the waters, take an evening or distance education course before you subscribe to a whole program. If you are having difficulty identifying your fears or figuring out how to approach them, talk to someone you trust. Ask for their recommendations, but always make your own personal decisions.

Oftentimes, simple visualizations, anchoring techniques, or self-hypnosis techniques can assist with removing challenging limitations and put you back in control of your plan. You can often find helpful free insight and tips for these techniques online or can obtain a free consultation from a local practioner for some more information. Just know that you always are in control of your decisions, actions, and limitations.

Without being honest with yourself you can't expect you'll better your life, you can only ask yourself these questions yet again until you find happiness.

Let me show you these questions in precise detail in the following diagram.

Who	What	Where	When	How
Who will I ask for help?	What do I want the outcome to be?	Where should I start?	When should I begin?	How should I begin?
Who will benefit from my career goal?	What will I do to get started?	Where will my career goal put me in 5 years?	When Do I want these goals to be reached?	How will these goals affect my future?
Who will I work with to accomplish my goal?	What will really make me happy?	Where will I apply my resources?	When will I apply my knowledge to begin attaining my goals?	How do I really feel about the goals?

Using an EZ guide Plan of Action Chart is such an essential tool to assist you in putting your plan into action and checking off your achievements as you accomplish them. I am sure you will want to refer to your own personal guide, that I am including a blank EZ Guide Plan of Action Chart at the back of this book for you to get started achieving your goals TODAY!

Here is a brief example showing Mary using the EZ Guide Plan of Action Chart. She is seeking a promotion at work and is using the chart to set her goal into action.

Completed	List Goal	Why is this important?	How can I accomplish this?	What can I do now?	Where will this happen?	When can I complete this?
✓	I want to get promoted at work	I deserve it and will make more $	I will make a to-do list	List ideas for improvement	I will do this in private	I will do this today!
✓	Need to get noticed at work	I can't move up if no one knows I'm there	Make a presentation	showing my idea for improvements	I will do this at work	Show it as soon as it is completed
	How can I let my work be seen	I know my work is good and strong	I will show my boss the presentation	My completed presentation for improvements	I will do this in my boss' office	I will do this when I know my boss can't ignore me

This is just a simplified sample showing how one would progress their plan of action. Mary would obviously continue on progressively as she successfully achieved each end goal and ultimately reaching her final goal of promotion or making changes if her direction in life changes.

In the same way you should follow the detail by detail methods mentioned in the above sections so that you can attain and maintain your established goals.   Just remember that you must develop an action plan if you are likely to succeed.

Tracking Your Progress

Simply by this stage, you probably have multiple lists of things to carry out and if it is essential, some plans for avoiding or working with potential challenges. Now you must put them all together directly into one comprehensive action plan. You must list tasks in the order which you need to complete them and set deadlines for your completion of any major ideas. Successful planners keep themselves on track using many different methods, such as

- Marking tasks on any monthly calendar (noting important dates for instance application deadlines, appointments, or action plans).
- Creating weekly or daily lists of activities and cross off tasks when they are completed.

- Using a pc program to create timeline charts which provide you time limits for task completion.
- Employing a commercial appointment book or any notebook; even a palm pilot using a new page for each evening or week.

Use whatever methods work best to suit your needs. Sometimes it is absolutely essential to ask a friend to check into your progress occasionally or question you on your own successes because you will be more motivated to get things done if you understand you'll be asked about them.

Now you have learned all that one could want to set successful goals. If you follow what exactly is in this section and have remembered the earlier sections, you will do just fine because you'll find nothing to hold you back today.

Creating Occupational Goals

One of toughest issues in making an excellent career choice and career setting goals is identifying what it is that you would like to do. Even when it seems you are aware what you want, you may still have doubts on if the career choice is the right choice for you.

Reaching clarity in those issues may be the most important thing you can do in your career planning and goal setting. Below are a few creative career goal setting guidelines which will help.

Most people, even very productive ones, have some periods along their career path when they seem to be unsure about their career selection and goals. It is totally human to think that way.

Often, such periods merely come and go. For illustration, they come when you face some overwhelming obstacles or challenges along your journey. It is all over when you get past these roadblocks or overcome the challenges.

That situation by itself is no hassle of choosing a career, just a test of your perseverance but imagine if those doubts persist, or if they always live somewhere in the back of your thoughts? If it just does not feel right?

If this could be the case, then it is time to focus more carefully on your career choice and overall career targets. Often you choose or are put in a career because it just may seem like the right step to make or it is what your studies have been dedicated to.

The only problem is that sometimes that passion that you once had as a young adult has dissipated, or the realism of the work has sapped the initial interest and joy you had right out of it.

That is when it is time to set a new career goal or objective. Choosing the right goal to sink into requires significant amounts of soul searching. You need to consider these questions beforehand:

1. Am I making the sort of money that I want to produce?

2. Do I want to earn more income?

3. Does money even matter?

4. Do I like what I'm doing today?

5. What am I zealous about?

6. What could I be doing that will make me happier than I will be right now?

7. Would I be happier simply switching positions or finding a promotion; or would I be happier changing careers completely?

8. Why am I working here?

9. What will be stopping me from leaving this kind of job?

10. What is stopping 'myself' from leaving this job?

These are all vital questions that you must ask yourself before deciding what your career goals will be. If you are really honest with yourself, you will know exactly what direction you need to be going in.

Creating Health/Fitness Goals

Setting a goal to become a member of an aerobics class and attend it 3 x per week makes the weight loss goal an integral part of your program. You will have set a target that is achievable almost right away. This gives you a perception of accomplishment, which is a reason to setting and achieving another goal.

Keeping Records

To begin, map out only eight weeks of activities toward your first fitness goal. Working inside your lifestyle, decide on a typical program. It's not necessary to work through every day, especially when beginning a fresh program as your body just isn't used to the stress. Your body becomes tired if expected to accomplish hard work seven days weekly.

Exercising every other day can be a safe and realistic goal. Record how much time you desire to spend doing an activity, accompanied by how much time you will actually devote to it.

Not everyone is looking at health and well-being to lose weight. Perhaps you might be just looking to better your quality of life.

In this case you should contemplate this; we tend to focus most around the area of our health inside our lives, when our health is failing or less than stellar.

Sadly, it may sometimes take a life threatening event, illness or some sort of physical rehabilitation to alert us to make tough changes inside our current health habits.

We make an effort to follow through on sound health principles, for instance; enough sleep, a healthy diet and a lot of exercise, yet we may not find the time in our schedules or have enough strength to implement a balanced and healthy lifestyle.

With the pressures within out fast pace world, stress can emerge and can take its toll. These days we are traveling more often. What that means is that we are eating while traveling as well, which doesn't always offer us the most effective or healthiest choices.

We are lucky to have six, maybe seven hours of sleep per night while we now work at least six days weekly. The old saying, "At least I have my health" finally means something to many people. You might be wondering how you could improve your health.

First thing to do is to prioritize what exactly is most important to your individual lifestyle. You can start with asking yourself these questions:

1. What exactly is my current exercise goal this month or should I even have one?

2. What keeps me from starting or continuing a balanced health maintenance system?

3. What's my target weight, my plan and/or timeframe?

3. How can my partner and I improve my sleeping habits?

5. What is my ideal appearance hopes?

6. Would a trainer, coach, or gym help me develop and reach my goals more effectively? Is this an affordable option?

7. Of the meals I eat monthly, how can I eat healthier, and what can I change so that I can eat healthier without getting bored to death?

8. What, how, or where can I study to improve upon my own health?

9. Is it time for me personally to go in for a whole physical and when was the last one?

10. How can my partner and I reduce or completely eliminate alcohol consumption, chemical dependencies and/or smoking within my body?

11. What ways could I manage to cook in a healthier way?

12. How can I improve my current heart rate, blood pressure, and cholesterol?

The fact is it doesn't matter what your fitness/health targets are. If you have read the sections on setting your goals targets effectively, and this section about health and well-being, you are ready to move into action.

You have to be honest with yourself at all times. When it comes to your personal goals, if you are unsure as to what constitutes good and balanced nutrition, visit this website http://www.choosemyplate.gov/ for the correct updated nutritional information.

> You should always consult with your family physician before making any changes to your diet or exercise regimen to ensure that you will not harm yourself.

Remember setting realistic goals are your stepping stones for success! That is all there is to it!

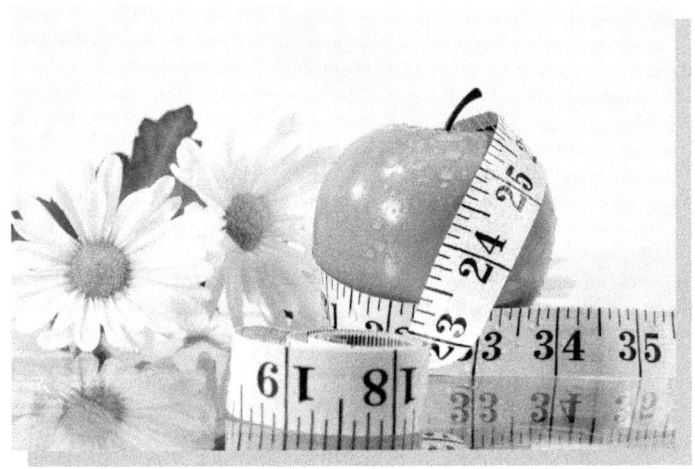

Creating Relationship Goals

For a relationship to be satisfying those associated with it must set clear goals. Most people go into relationships having a vague idea of what they want from the partnership. When pressed, they often are unable to be able to specify their goals for the relationship ultimately.

Goals can be stated or perhaps written, but they should be arranged by the partners in the beginning of the relationship. Relationship targets sometimes are dictated by habits. However, for a relationship to be effective and successful, the goals stated should be only those where both partners can agree.

The partnership goal should be kept in a safe place and reviewed, as our needs have a tendency to change. During the annual review the goals may be modified, and the objectives being achieved for the next year may be identified.

Relationship goals should be lasting, but they should be general enough to offer the partners enough latitude being satisfying and easy to attain. Annual objectives based on these goals may be more specific and short expression, motivating the partners to successfully achieving them inside each year.

Relationship goals should be produced to cover key issues mixed up in their relationship, but they can cover any part of human behavior. In order to best discover how and what goals must be set, you have to ask yourself many different questions to get to know yourself along with your partner.

Here is a little eye-opening quiz:

<u>Relationship Goals Quiz</u>

1. How can we best nurture our support for each other?

2. How will we communicate with one another on a regular basis?

3. How dependent will we be toward the other person and is it healthy?

4. How can we give our mutual intimacy a fresh start in this relationship?

5. What length of time do we intend our relationship status to last; as an example, do we want to marry on specified date or continue on as partners?

6. How will we make certain that we respect each other's rights in this relationship?

7. How will we assist the other person's "growth" in this relationship?

8. How do we keep the 'fun' inside our relationship?

9. How will we include others inside our relationship without losing our support for each other?

10. How will we approach challenges inside our relationship?

11. How will we resolve problems?

12. How will we handle disagreements?

13. How will we handle irritating annoyances and is it worth the time and effort?

14. How are we planning to handle fights and bring these to a healthy resolution?

15. At what point will we seek help for ourselves if our fighting gets out of control or will we even take the time, for example will we find counseling together?

16. Will we consent to disagree?

17. How can we ensure mutual growth in this relationship?

18. How open are we to accepting joint and individual responsibility for our relationship?

19. How can we make certain that our individuality doesn't get lost in this relationship?

20. How open are we to being assertive inside our relationship?

21. How can we use our unique, individual personalities to aid each other and cultivate our relationship?

22. What steps will we acquire if one or both partners ever feels smothered by the relationship?

23. What steps are we ready to take if one or both partners needs emotional health assistance?

24. How are we planning to promote each other's physical health and will we be supportive of each other?

25. What steps can we use to handle jealousy, competition, or resentment toward the other person?

26. How are we going to manage our time to do all that we want to do?

29. How are we going to manage our schedules so that we could pursue our unique, individual interests whilst still spend quality time together?

28. How free are we to be able to pursue our distinct interests and also friends?

29. How committed are we to creating long range relationship goals and short range objectives to succeed in those goals?

30. How committed are we to creating times in which we can nourish the other person and keep our relationship on course?

31. How can we structure techniques for getting the "required" relationship maintenance jobs.

32. How can we delegate the maintenance tasks so that neither individual is left feeling like they are doing all the work?

33. What place will religion, interests, sports, and outside interests have inside our relationship?

34. How important are those ideas to our relationship?

35. How easily can we negotiate and resolve our differences?

I know that this sounds like plenty of questions, but seriously; if you are realistic, all of these inquiries matter. If you cannot actually take this little quiz seriously; how can you expect to take the relationship seriously?

How your relationship scored:

For every same response give yourselves 1 point, and for each and every different answer, take 1 point away.

If you and your spouse score below 17, that doesn't mean that you need to break up, it just means that the two of you have to sit down and determine your personal relationship goals with each other and form a compromise you could both agree with.

All relationships require compromise by both parties if it's going to succeed. You just need to re-evaluate what your goals will be. Mutually agree on those new goals, and you will find that your relationship will be even more successful.

If you and your spouse scored above 17, it simply means that you are on the right course and are likely looking to obtain the same things out of the partnership. You will still have to compromise somewhat (you are human) to maintain the relationship going, but you are heading in the right direction.

What you need to understand is that setting relationship goals is most beneficial when both parties get excited about the process. If only you are working for the betterment of the relationship, it is doomed to be unsuccessful anyway because one partner will always feel overworked inside the relationship. You have control only of your own wants and desires. You cannot force your control onto others. Your partner will have control over his/her goals. Success comes by mutually working towards the same agreed upon goals

Setting relationship goals is not any different than setting up any other type of goal. The largest difference is you generally have to set your goals with each other being in agreement. Setting relationship goals benefit all types of relationships; friendships, family relationships, fellow workers or partners.

You can make an effort to set the goals and work with them yourself, but it will probably be very difficult and quite unfulfilling. That is why the importance to setting relationship goals is to offer full co-operation and support to those whose relationships you desire the most.

Other than that, you can merely follow the steps by way of achieving your goals as mentioned in the section entitled, "Establishing Goals: Plan of Action".

Creating
Financial / Money Goals

Step one in personal financial planning is learning how to control your day-to-day financial affairs to enable you to do the things that allow you to get satisfaction and enjoyment. This is achieved by planning and using a budget.

The second step inside personal financial planning, and the main focus of this section, is choosing and using a plan toward achieving your long-term economic goals.

As with anything different in life, without financial targets and specific plans for achieving them, you will just move along and leave your upcoming to chance. A wise person once said: "Most people don't want to fail; they just fail to be able to plan." The end result is the same and it's also a failure for you to reach economic independence.

The third step in private financial planning is developing a financial safety net, which is like creating a retirement fund for when you are no longer generating any revenue. This will allow you to enjoy the rewards of your achievements.

FOUR EZ STEPS FOR ESTABLISHING FINANCIAL GOALS

Step 1: Identify and take note of your financial goals, whether they are saving to send your kids to university, buying a new car, saving to get a down payment on a residence, going on vacation, paying off personal credit card debt, or planning for retirement.

Step 2: Break each financial goal into several short-term (less than 1 year), medium-term (1 - 3 years) and long-term (5 years or more) goals; which is likely to make this process easier.

Step 3: Educate yourself and research before you buy. Read finance magazines or any book about investing, or surf the Internet's investment sites. Do not be afraid with the stock or mutual fund markets. Take advantage of employer matching programs. Talk with your Human Resources department. Never be afraid to ask foolish questions if there is something you do not understand! Only fools, never ask!

Yes, there can be a potential for loss, but with your research and getting a trustworthy broker, you can make strides toward securing your financial future. Just remember not to put your entire eggs in one basket.

Diversify your portfolio. With a little effort it is possible to learn enough to make educated decisions that may increase your net worth over time. Then identify small, measurable actions you can take to achieve these goals, and put this step plan to work.

Step 4: Evaluate your progress as needed. Review your development monthly, quarterly, or at any interval you feel comfortable with, but at least semi-annually, to ascertain if your program is functioning properly. Always remember your goals and that you are responsible to make sure your plan of action is set in motion.

If you're not making an effective amount of progress on a certain goal, re-evaluate your approach and also make changes as necessary.

There are not any 'cast in stone' rules for implementing an economic plan. The important thing is to be doing something, rather than nothing, and to start **TODAY**.

Sometimes when people write down their goals, they discover that a number of the goals are too broad in meaning and extremely hard to reach, while others might appear smaller in scope and better to achieve.

It is okay to dare to dream about riches, but be realistic about what you can do. Yes, you could become a successful millionaire, if that is your goal. Most of the wealthiest and most successful individuals in the world reached that acclaim by successfully accomplishing set goals. Just realize that realistically, there will be many steps on that ladder to reach that point. A good idea is always to break your goals down into three separate timeframes.

One more thing to keep in mind: by placing a time frame on your own goals you are motivating yourself to begin and helping to allow you the chance to succeed. Just remember that you can easily adjust the time frame whenever you would like to.

Long-term goals (over 5 years) are those ideas that won't happen overnight, irrespective of how hard you work to accomplish them.

They may take quite a while to accomplish (hence the reason they may be called long term goals), so give yourself a reasonable timeframe, estimate based on your experience or knowledge of how long it may take to achieve them.

Examples of long-term goals might include college education, having a child, retirement plan or buying a home. Whatever the case, these goals generally require more time commitments and often more money in the long run.

Intermediate-term goals (1-5 years) are the sort of goals that can't be executed overnight but may not take many years to attain. Examples might include purchasing/replacing a vehicle, getting an education or qualification, or paying off your debts like bank cards etc. (depending on the amount).

Short-term goals (within one year) generally take 12 months or less to achieve, best to date the task, the total estimated cost, as well as the required savings, as necessary.

What are your goals? To find out, you should make up a list, determine which timeline your goal matches into, detail the steps required to achieve your goals, then you act toward reaching those goals. It's that simple.

You might be wondering the place to start when deciding how to begin your financial targets. Here are some basic tips to assist you in choosing the best options for you.

After looking at these guidelines, it is best for you to do some research to get the method(s) that suit your own individual needs.

- Use coupons. It may seem like small savings, but add together you might save 20-30 dollars each visit to the market.

- Shop around regarding bargains or sales.

- Begin by taking 5%-10% away from each pay check and input it in a savings account.

- Look into different investment strategies for instance IRA's, stocks, RRSP's, mutual Resources, personal investments etc. There are many more and all will help you in short and long expression goals.

- Do not live outside your current means.

- Work with a credit counselor to have help in lowering your monthly expenses and remove your past debt.

These are just some of the things you can do when beginning to realize your financial goals. Of course, there are also steps inside the earlier sections on how to be able to successfully set goals.

The methods to setting goals successfully don't modify, only the methods that you employ to go about it. By that I mean; when it is job wise, work to get seen; for relationships, work on maintaining your intimacy; in financial matters, work to save lots of money etc. It is actually that easy.

Creating Family Goals

Every family could use a small amount of help in setting family goals. Perhaps your family wants to go on a really fantastic vacation together; that three day romantic getaway only for the parents that never seems to come about; or the home improvement project no one ever seems to have time for.

Most families are now living on a limited budget. Living within that budget can help your household pay off those credit cards forever and realize your child's dreams of college or your dream of getting a bigger and better residence.

Perhaps your family's goal is to see your kids go from a 'C' average to a 'B' or to have quality family time together. Maybe you want to commence your own home-based business to enable you to spend more time with your family at home.

Each and every one of these brilliant worthy goals can be easily achieved in a somewhat remarkable and FUN approach.

In fact, you may discover how working toward a goal, may be more fun than achieving that particular goal. If you desire to add some real teamwork within your family and deepen your familial interactions, you must set goals along with your whole family together.

Just make sure that anyone who participates with the goal setting process is motivated enough to follow through with the plan of action. Anyone who is not fully focused on achieving the goal really should not be allowed to participate or reap the rewards.

If you really want to instruct your kids in something worthwhile that can help them with every aspect of their lives, teach them how to set goals successfully.

Here's the goal-setting system that generally seems to work for everyone who has experimented with it. It will work with basically any goal you can imagine and especially, family goals you can achieve together.

It is a powerful way to get the whole family working together toward a successful plan of action and a specific set goal. If nothing else, your family will have an enjoyable experience trying.

1. Dream it.

Make a list of precisely what you each think you need... all the goals you think you would like to achieve. They may involve funds, or material things, or far better relationships, or a special getaway, or a change in your own personal attitudes or habits.

Get paper and a pen and go somewhere to be completely alone and uninterrupted. Write down everything, being careful not to judge or dismiss any ideas. Remember that everyone in the family should do this. You will all compare and compromise on which goals will be most effective to work towards achieving first.

After you have this long list written down, put the list away for a couple days. Some of the things you wrote down may begin creating a burning energy in your head.

Review your list in a week and see which goals you're still interested in. Remove anything that you don't feel strongly about from the list. Goal setting will not work if you are not really motivated to that goal. Have your family members do the same.

After you identify the goal or goals that you would like to work on, start writing everything down. A notebook only for your goals might be beneficial. Write down your goals on the first page of your notebook and you may all start determining which goals are least to most critical.

2. Identify the obstacles

After you've set the goal, make a list of items that may threaten the successful good results of the goal and what you can do to remove those threats.

As an example, are you and your husband or wife or child fighting over many of these goals? Write down ALL the obstacles which you feel may prevent you from reaching your goal.

Once the obstacles are usually clearly defined, they are most of the time, easily resolved.

3. Identify things that will help.

After you've identified the road blocks, make a written list with the things you will need to experience your goal.

This list should include the people whose cooperation can assist you work toward your goal. A number of the items on this list can include some things that will represent answers to the problems you wrote down earlier.

4. Set a date.

Setting a date for the attainment of one's goal is the ignition for the goal-seeking missile in your head. Make sure that your time is realistic... not so soon that it is impossible, but not so delayed that it is not interesting.

Make sure you write the completion date for the goal down next to the goal. Once you've set this kind of date, you should never change it unless it is absolutely essential.

5. Goal Reminders.

Once you have your goal and the date written, make more reminders of the goal. Put these reminders all over your house, on the fridge, in the bathroom or in the car.

Notes or postings will remind you of the goal and the date the goal will be achieved, and each time you see this information you will end up programming your mind to act toward your goal. This can be an important step.

Creating Artistic Goals

Are you the sort of person that always admired the creative and artistic people within the world like singers, actors, copy writers, poets, and painters? Have you always wondered what masterpieces you might create if you only had enough time or skills? Have you struggled with your artistic pursuits? Limited yourself with believing that all artist, must starve?

Chances are if you want to set artistic goals, do you have the passion, interest, and skills. If not, perhaps part of your goal is to attend school for it.

Whatever the reason why or what skill level you have reached, you too can create a great artistic achievement. Many individuals limit their creative goals believing that talent is a born trait. Creativity can be developed, learned, and achieved by goal setting.

Before trying to accomplish your artistic goals, you should first ensure that you know all of the steps necessary to begin. You should also know what your own personal skill level is so you can begin chasing your artistic goal on the right course from the beginning.

Ask yourself these questions before:

1. What style of fine art most interests me: illustration, music, painting, writing etc.?

2. What is my current ability?

3. Do I want to pursue it as a hobby or create income?

4. Do I need to attend school or a training course?

5. Am I looking for certification or perhaps basic techniques or skills?

6. Do I have the time to attend school or a training course?

7. Do I want to relieve stress? or create a masterpiece or salable work?

8. How much does this mean to me if you ask me?

9. Is this really something that I must pursue?

10. Will doing this make me happy?

When creating artistic goals, you must follow the chunking down step by steps method in the above sections. The most important thing you can do to help you set and reach your artistic goals is to adhere to it.

That's right; the best thing you can do to achieve your artistic goals is always to just persevere.

Art consists of 90% creative ideas and 10% perspiration. Just inspire yourself the best way that suits you uniquely. If you follow The EZ guide and maintain your focus on your goals, you can succeed creatively!

.

Get Motivated

How could I write helpful tips to setting and achieving success if I didn't actually offer you a few tips on the most critical part of setting goals?

The main element to successful goal setting can be your ability to motivate yourself and stay motivated to successfully achieve your goals. Getting and staying motivated is not as difficult as it may seem. It just takes self-control. Let's look at the factors that you should acquire to stay motivated.

First, let's have a look at what motivation really is.

- Motivation isn't a product of an outside effect; it is a natural product of one's desire to achieve something and your belief that you will be capable of doing it.

- Positive goals that are geared toward your pleasure are much better motivators than negative ones that are derived from fear.

Now let's look at what you could do to motivate yourself and maintain that state.

1. Start with really visualizing your upcoming success and model those feelings you'll experience once you achieve it.

2. Mentally walk the path toward this success and experience the feelings at different milestones along the way.

3. Assign a high priority to each task you have to achieve, which will give each task a priority in your conscious and subconscious mind.

4. Set a target for how much work you will do daily toward your goals.

5. Visualize the specified outcome: Create a picture of what the specified outcome will look like.

6. Use visual indicators to monitor your progress and complete the tasks.

7. Give yourself affirmations to point out to yourself how capable you are at reaching your goals (written, verbal, or mental).

8. View movies/tv shows/books that motivate you.

9. Listen to music that motivates you.

10. Imagine an individual you really want to emulate, real or fictional in front of you. Visualize stepping forward and blending into their image, experience those qualities that you want to possess.

11. In the event you have a competitive nature, make a deal with a friend to compete for the goal.

12. Get assistance and support coming from people around you or from a professional; as an example a personal trainer, finance director etc.

13. Define your very own version of 'success', don't allow others to create their definitions for you.

14. Ignore any negative influences or comments in your efforts.

15. Make a conscious effort to accomplish better than you have ever done before.

16. Focus on the positive achievements rather than the negatives.

17. Share your successes with others as this will allow you to stay focused and will give voice to your accomplishments. You will realize your achievements increasing your self-esteem and confidence.

18. Acknowledge your strengths and weaknesses. Work with them both to blend together a working strategy for success. (Example: You have a weakness of shutting off your alarm clock, going back to sleep and being late to work! Obviously, your body is tired. Your strengths need to negotiate with this weakness. Either, go to bed earlier, move the clock further away, etc... strengths/weakness work together for a solution.)

19. Train yourself to finish what you start by refusing to give up until you are done.

20. Don't forget humans do make mistakes and don't punish yourself when you make them. Extract useful learning experiences to apply to your future goals.

Goal Establishing: Do's and Don'ts

For the purposes of this guide I thought a good do's and don'ts category can help you get to the nitty-gritty in the nice and quick manner. Contemplate it; if you are reading this, you want to start establishing goals and achieving them now, not later. This can be an instant guide for re-reading later.

Do's	Don'ts
Visualize your desired outcome	Begin with "I can't do this" attitude
Think positive all the time	Be overcome by negatives or set backs
Write down your Plan of Action in an EZ step-by-step format	Try to memorize all of the steps
Begin Plan of Action upon knowing what you want	Procrastinate, make excuses for your delaying
Learn to organize your thought patterns	Let anything stand in your way of achieving your goals

Be specific in your goals	Set goals that are too vague
Be realistic in your setting your goals	Set your goals too high to achieve them
Surround yourself with motivating factors	Forget why you set goal in first place
Keep track of all of your achievements	Downplay your achievements
Share your successful achievements	Let yourself get off track, lose your focus

Achieving Goals with Time Management

Effectively achieving goals begins with time management. You must be able to balance your time and energy in the best way possible to experience your goals. Most of us don't achieve goals because we "lack the particular time". That is why I knew this section would have to be included in this guide.

The concept of time management has been in existence for more than 100 years contrary to popular belief. Unfortunately the term "Time management" generates a false impression of what you were able to do.

Time cannot be managed, time is uncontrollable and we could only manage ourselves and our usage of time. That is all that can be done. Time management is actually a do-it-yourself management.

For effective time management we need the opportunity to plan, delegate, organize, direct and control all facets of our lives just to get 30 minutes a day for our own personal special use.

There are common time wasters which must be identified.

In order for your time management process to work, you will need to know what aspects of your personal management must be improved. Otherwise what is the purpose in trying?

Below you will find one of the most frequent reasons. You might desire to check the ones which are being the major obstacles in your own personal time management. These are called your time and energy stealers.

Identifying your time and energy stealers

- Interruptions, for example: phone calls, friends or TV

- Meetings

- Procrastination and indecision

- Acting devoid of total information

- Dealing with someone else's issues or problems

- Some type of personal crisis, for example, relative is sick or injured.

- Inadequate knowledge

- Unclear objectives and / or priorities

- Lack of planning

- Stress, anxiety, nervousness and fatigue

- Inability to say "No" to anyone's requests

- Personal disorganization

You know there are many more that I didn't list, isn't there? Fortunately, there are strategies you can use to manage your time in an easier way and be better able to handle and reduce stress. You can analyze your time and energy seeing how you may well be both the cause and the perfect solution to your time challenges.

We will look at time management issues in more depth.

1. **Shifting priorities and problems management**. Crisis management, dealing with an issue as it occurs, actually takes longer to resolve and consumes more time in tracking where it originally began. Actions taken ahead of the crisis could have prevented it from the beginning.

2. Cell phone and other social media. Have you ever had one particular day when you just seemed to answer the phone with "Grand Central Station, how can I assist you?" The phone can become our greatest communication tool but may be our biggest enemy to effectiveness unless you know how to control its hold over you. Emails, chat sites and other social media can toss our time right out the door. Before we realize it, time has swept us by and we are rushing to catch up.

3. Not enough priorities/objectives. This is probably the greatest and one of the most important time wasters. This affects all we do equally professionally and personally. Those who accomplish the most in one day know exactly what they desire to accomplish beforehand.

Unfortunately, many think that goals and objectives are yearly things rather than daily considerations. This usually results in too much effort spent on the minor things rather than on the things which are very important to our daily present lives.

4. Attempting to take on the world. Many people today feel that they must accomplish everything yesterday and don't give themselves sufficient time to do things properly. This leads only to half-finished projects and no feeling of achievement. All things are done on the fly.

5. Drop in visitors. The five deadliest words that rob your time and energy are "Have you got a minute?" Everyone does it; fellow workers, the boss, your peers, and your family and friends.

Knowing how to deal with these interruptions is probably the best skill you can acquire and understand.

6. Ineffective delegation. Good delegation is known as a key skill, equally in managers and successful leaders.

The best managers have a power to delegate work to staff and family members to ensure it gets done correctly. This is probably the simplest way of building a team's spirit and reducing your own workload concurrently.

The general rule; if one of your people can do it 80% as well as you can, delegate it.

8. Procrastination. The greatest thief of time is not necessarily decision making but decision prevention. Reducing the amount of procrastinating you are doing can substantially increase how much active time is available to each individual.

9. The inability to say "no!" The general principle is; if people can dump their work or problems on your shoulders they will do so quite happily, time and time again.

Some of the most pressured people around, lack the talent to 'just say no', due to their anxiety about upsetting people. Get over it because these individuals can do it for themselves or find someone else more often than not.

10. Meetings. Studies have shown the average professional person spends about 17 hours weekly in meetings, about 6 hours in planning and untold hours in just the follow up process of those meetings.

Time Management Strategies

There are many ways we could manage our time. I have listed some strategies you need to manage your time better and in a more efficient way.

1. Always define your goals as clearly as you can.

Do you find you are not doing what you should be doing, just because your goals never been set properly yet?

One of the many factors which make successful people noticeable is their ability to work through what they want to achieve. They often possess written goals which they can easily review constantly.

Your goals should have an impact on your activities and be included on your "to do" list.

2. Analyze your usage of time.

Are you spending enough time on the projects which may not be urgent now, but are things you need to do to develop yourself or your career?

If you are constantly thinking about "What can I do to make things easier for me today?" it will help you to spotlight 'important tasks' and stop re-acting to tasks which just seem important (or pleasant to do) yet carry no importance towards your goals.

3. Have a plan.

How will you achieve your goals without an idea? I don't even think that's possible. Most people know what they desire but have no plan to accomplish it except by sheer work. What's the point in doing work when you don't learn how to apply it?

Your yearly plan needs to be reviewed and reset as soon as your achievements are met. Successfully productive people make lists constantly.

It enables them to stay together with priorities and enables them to keep flexible to changing their priorities. This can easily be done for both personal and business goals.

4. Actions plan analysis.

Problems will always happen once you set a plan into motion. The value of having your good plan of action is to identify problems early and search for solutions immediately.

Good time management allows you to measure your progress towards your goals because "What's possible to measure, you can control".

Always be positive and proactive in the achievement of successfully managing your time and energy.

Time management is not a difficult subject to understand, but until you are committed to building far better time management techniques into your daily routine, you'll only attain partial (or no) results and find yourself right back where you started out.

You have to commit to managing your time and energy better and remember to include time for yourself.

By setting goals and removing time wasters, you will have extra time in the week to spend on the individuals and activities most important for you to live a more abundantly successful life.

Controlling Stress
For Success

Stress management wouldn't seem like something that would take part in creating goals but it may be the difference between you achieving them and never achieving them.

There is good stress and negative stress. Positive stress adds anticipation and excitement, and we all thrive under some stress. Deadlines, competitions, confrontations, as well as our frustrations and sorrows add depth and enrichment to our lives.

Our goal is not to get rid of stress but to learn to manage it and how to use it so that it will help you achieve your goals. Insufficient stress acts like a depressant and may leave a person feeling bored or dejected; however, excessive stress may leave you feeling all confused and anxious.

What you need is to find the optimal degree of stress that will motivate you without overwhelming you.

What is your personal optimal stress level?

There is no single degree of stress that is optimal for everyone. We are all individual beings with are own unique requirements. What is distressing to one can be a joy to another. If we agree that a specific event is distressing, we will probably differ in each of our physiological and psychological responses to it. That's just human nature.

Each individual's brain will process the information it receives uniquely. Not only will you have the physical chemical response, but your subconscious perspective will place its stamp on it too.

The one who loves to arbitrate disputes as well as moves from job site to job site will be stressed in a job which was stable and routine, whereas the one who thrives under a more stable condition would most likely be stressed on a job where duties were highly diverse or mobile.

Your personal stress requirements and the amount that you can endure before becoming distressed changes as you age. It has been found that many illnesses are related to unrelieved tension; for example, anxiety disorders, intestinal disorders etc.

If you tend to be experiencing stress symptoms, you have gone above your optimal stress level; you need to reduce the stress that you are experiencing and/or improve your ability to handle it.

Stress symptoms include, but aren't limited to:

- Hair loss

- Anxiety attacks

- Headaches

- Fatigue

- Lack of appetite

- Increase of appetite

How can you manage stress?

Identifying unrelieved stress and being conscious of its effect on your life isn't sufficient for reducing its dangerous effects. Just as there are many causes of stress, there are many possibilities towards its management.

However, all require work to become effective. Changing the source of stress and/or changing your reaction to it. How can you do that? Let me demonstrate.

1. Become aware of your stressors as well as your emotional and physical reactions.

- Notice your stress and its beginnings. Don't ignore it. Do not gloss over your problems.

- Determine exactly what events stress you out. Just how much do these events mean for you?

- Determine how your body responds towards the stress. Do you become anxious or physically upset? If you do, in what specific ways?

2. Recognize what you can alter.

- Can you change your stressors through avoiding or eliminating them totally?

- Can you reduce their intensity with time?

- Can you shorten your contact with stress by taking a break, or physically leaving?

- Can you devote the time and effort necessary to altering this reaction (goal setting, time management methods, counseling, anchoring, and/or delayed gratification strategies might be helpful here)?

3. Reduce the intensity your emotional reactions to stress.

The strained reaction is triggered by your own perception of danger, worries, physical danger, emotional threat, fears of failure, etc.

- Are you viewing your stressors in exaggerated terms and/or going for a difficult situation and making it into a tragedy?

- Are you expecting to please everyone? I'm telling you honestly that you will never please everyone. So just release that stressor, as soon as possible.

- Are you overreacting and considering things as absolutely 'critical and urgent', constantly? Do you feel you should always come out the winner in most situations?

- Work at adopting more moderate views; try to begin to see the stress as something you can deal with rather than something that overpowers you.

- Try to temper your extreme emotions. Try imagining the situation from a different perspective. Do not labor on the negative facet of everything, find a positive aspect.

- Take a deep breath when overly anxious and count backwards from 10.

- Exercise a bit or take a walk every day.

5. Build your physical supplies.

- Eat healthy, well-balanced, and nutritious meals.

- Maintain your own ideal weight or appearance.

- Avoid smoking, excessive caffeine, and alcohol.

- Mix leisure time with work. Take breaks and get away when you are able.

- Take 5 seconds to just close your eyes, slowly breathe through your nose, and relax the tension pressure behind your eyes.

- Get enough sleep. Keeping a regular sleep and wake schedule eases the stress reaction response in your body.

6. Maintain your emotional supplies.

- Develop some mutually supportive friendships/relationships.

- Pursue realistic goals that are meaningful to you, rather than goals others believe you should be fulfilling.

- Expect some frustrations, failures, as well as sorrows and allow them to proceed.

- Always be kind and gentle with yourself. Be your own personal best friend.

Portable Anchoring Technique: Energy of Excellence

Purpose: I wanted to include this anchoring technique. It is an extremely useful and portable tool that I use and advise my clients on how to apply in their lives. It is a simple exercise that you can instantly access when needed.

Many individuals use anchoring techniques, some by their knowledge of application and others, do so without realizing it. Perhaps, they have a lucky charm, affirmation, mantra...etc. Anchoring is a great non-hypnotic tool for achieving your set goals successfully.

1. Creating the Energy of Excellence: Imagine a circle on the floor in front of you. See it in your mind, what does it look like? Round? Cylinder? Flat? What color is it? How does it feel? Are there any sounds inside it? Create this circle in any way that you choose, it is just for yourself.

2. Imagine having a resource tool for yourself. What energy of excellence would you want to have <u>more</u> of in your lifetime? More Motivation? Self-confidence? Success? Etc. Imagine

you have resources available to you that enable you to apply these traits and protect you. "

3. Now, remember a time when you had experienced this trait. Pretend you are there today. When you are fully experiencing how that feels, step into the circle you created on the floor.

4. Then, step back out of the circle, leaving that state of excellence there. Relax.

5. Now, step back into you circle, and notice just how that feels now.

Note: If the response just isn't as strong as you desire, you can add other resources at this point by repeating steps 3, 4, and 5.

6. Anchoring is the key: First, you will need to think of a time or situation where you desire to have more of this distinct trait of excellence.   When you begin to access this previously unresourceful event, step forward in to your circle.   Imagine the energy of excellence flowing all around you dissipating that negative energy. Enjoy the state of excellence.

Where might that situation occur once more? or What happens now once you think of what used to look wrong?

Creatively think of ways to bring your circle with you to be automatically available in lots of other situations as needed.

Suggestions: inside your heart, behind an ear, beneath your watch, perhaps, set within a ring on your finger, etc. Imagine how having these resources now will be useful in your future situations.

Summary

Now that you have read this entire guide you've learned the skills that you'll need in order to design and achieve every one of the goals that you written down for yourself. In this guide, you have learned:

- How to create a successful goal setting strategy.

- How to create goals effectively.

- How to cope with stress that can hinder your time and efforts.

- How to motivate yourself.

- How to set realistic goals in all aspects in your life.

- How to manage your time toward successfully achieving your set goals.

- A step-by-step chunking down method for creating a plan of action to achieving your goals.

- How to create a portable Energy of Excellence that you can use as a resource tool as needed, when needed.

- How to use the EZ guide diagram chart to map out your goals and track your achievements.

Hopefully you've realized just how EZ it can be to achieving your goals, if you set your mind to it.

Setting goals properly doesn't need to be the most difficult thing that can be done because it can be really stimulating. If you challenge yourself correctly and set time aside to create your goals you can complete them successfully.

You have learned that procrastination is your enemy when trying to achieve something and you have learned how goals can be set for almost every aspect of your existence; including family, relationships, finances, company, health/fitness etc.

Why should you waste your time and effort dreaming and hoping for a better life when you are able go and successfully attain your dreams one goal at a time? You don't need to know anything more to get started, besides what you have learned here on the way to your more successful and fulfilling future.

Today is the beginning of your journey to achieving all of your goals and realizing your dreams successfully!

EZ Guide Plan of Action Chart

Completed	List Goal	Why is this important?	How can I accomplish this?	What can I do now?	Where will this happen?	When can I complete this?

Appendix

I am a certified Neuro-linguistics practioner, life coach and hypnotist. I am a member with the American Alliance of Hypnotists and American University of NLP.

I reside in South Haven, Michigan. I also am the successful owner of www.creativeconsciousconcepts.com which allows me to reach out globally and motivate more individuals to take control of their lives and realize that they can achieve their dreams.

My client base consists largely of people who need to lose weight, stop smoking or gain confidence. Other clients include individuals interested in boosting their motivation and increasing their income, overcoming shyness, or job placement focus, to name just a few topics.

It is my hope that this book will inspire you to take that first step and start achieving your desired goals today. As I firmly believe this EZ guide will bring you success in all areas of your life. I can assure you, you would not be reading this book if it were not for the benefits of goal setting in my own life being applied.

It was an EZ choice for me to decide that this book's focus would be the most valuable and beneficial to others. I have found purpose in my life and I want to be able to share with others how they can easily achieve the successful lives that they desire.

For more information about me or on achieving your set goals successfully, you are welcome to explore and visit my website, Www.creativeconsciousconcepts.com .

There, you will find a collection of Self-Hypnosis Audios, Life Coaching, Anchoring Techniques and other self-improvement articles / tips.

You also will find a link to my e-mail address:

Cynthia@creativeconsciousconcepts.com

I am available to answer your questions or address your concerns, and I wish you all the success, happiness and prosperity the world has to offer.

www.ingramcontent.com/pod-product-compliance
Lightning Source LLC
Chambersburg PA
CBHW070157290526
45789CB00002B/808